My 1st Book of Eclipses

Sara Kale

Amazon Page: amazon.com/author/sarakale
Email: sara.rainbowartsstudio@gmail.com
IG: rainbow_artsstudio

What is an Eclipse?

An eclipse is a special natural event that occurs when one heavenly body passes through the shadow of another. On earth, we observe two main types: solar eclipses, where the sun appears dark, and lunar eclipses, where the moon appears dark.

>>> Solar Eclipse

>>> Lunar Eclipse

What is a Solar Eclipse?

A solar eclipse happens when the moon moves between earth and the sun, blocking the sun's light and casting its shadow on earth, causing darkness during the day.

sun

moon

earth

Partial Solar Eclipse

During a partial solar eclipse, the moon covers part of the sun, making it look like a crescent. This makes the sun appear to have a missing piece, shaped like the moon.

crescent sun   moon

Total Solar Eclipse

During a total solar eclipse, the moon covers the sun, making it dark. We can see a super hot, glowing halo around the sun. It's called the Corona, which is the sun's outer atmosphere.

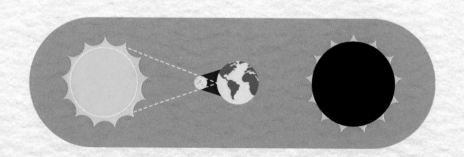

corona

moon

Annular Solar Eclipse

During an annular solar eclipse, the moon doesn't completely cover the sun because it is farther away from earth and appears smaller. This creates a beautiful ring of sunlight around the edges.

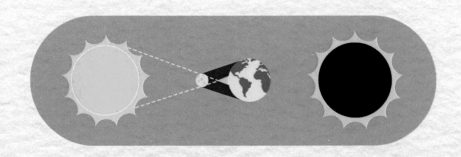

moon

sun

Solar Eclipse Safety

No Staring at the sun

Never look directly at the sun. It's too bright and can hurt your eyes.

Use Eclipse Glasses

If you want to watch the eclipse, wear special eclipse glasses only. These glasses keep your eyes safe.

Make Fun DIY Projectors

You can also make cool projectors with cardboard boxes to see the eclipse without looking at the sun.

Solar Eclipse Safety

Keep Pets Inside

Even pets should stay inside during an eclipse because their eyes can get hurt too.

Listen to Grown-Ups

Always listen to adults or teachers about how to watch an eclipse safely.

Remember, safety first!

What is a Lunar Eclipse?

A lunar eclipse happens when the earth comes between the sun and the moon, blocking sunlight and casting a shadow on the moon. This makes the moon look darker or sometimes even change color.

Partial Lunar Eclipse

During a partial lunar eclipse, only a part of the moon moves through earth's shadow, so it appears partially darkened.

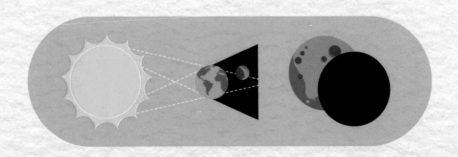

earth's shadow

Total Lunar Eclipse

During a total lunar eclipse, the earth completely covers the moon, causing it to appear red or orange, commonly known as a "blood moon".

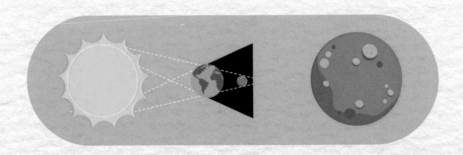

blood moon

"Blood Moon"

A 'blood moon' looks red or orange because sunlight slips through the earth's air or atmosphere, coloring the moon in shades of red or orange.

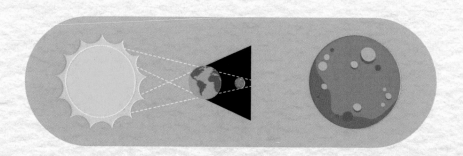

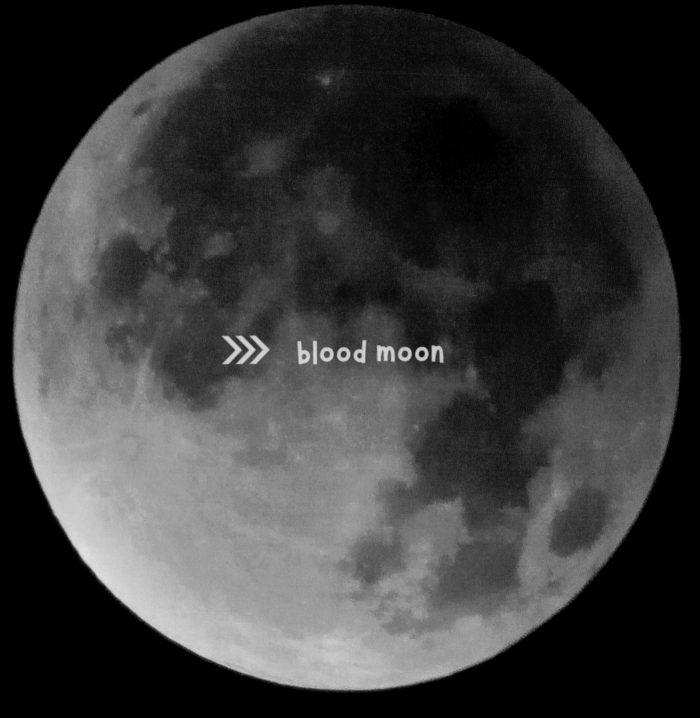

Penumbral Lunar Eclipse

During a penumbral lunar eclipse, the moon passes through the earth's outer shadow called the penumbra. This makes the moon appear a bit less bright.

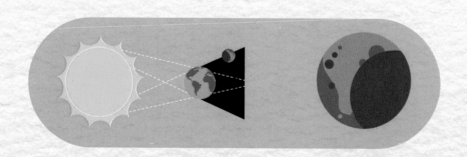

earth's shadow makes the moon look less bright

Activity

&

Fun Facts

Fun Fact # 1

A solar leafy shadow is a cool thing that happens during a solar eclipse. When the moon covers part of the sun, the sunlight peeking through the small spaces between tree leaves makes lots of tiny crescent shaped shadows on the ground.

Fun Fact # 2

During a solar eclipse, when it gets dark and cooler, animals act like it's night time. Birds might nap and stop singing, bees may go back to their hive, crickets may start chirping, cows might head to the barn, and night animals like bats and owls may wake up and do their usual activities.

Match The Correct Eclipse Name

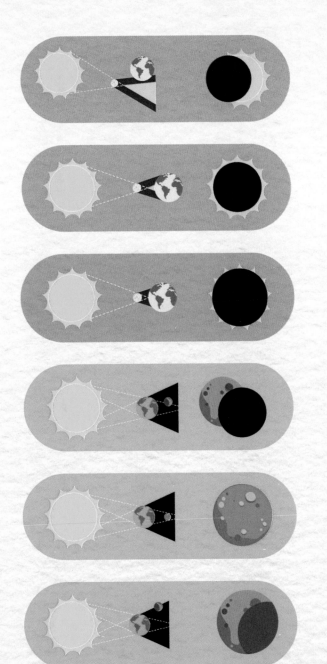

Total Solar Eclipse

Penumbral Lunar Eclipse

Partial Solar Eclipse

Total Lunar Eclipse

Annular Solar Eclipse

Partial Lunar Eclipse

Made in the USA
Las Vegas, NV
08 April 2024